Terrific Toddlers

or Tantrum Free Two's - Almost!

By Mel Hayde

Terrific Toddlers
(Tantrum Free Two's - Almost!)

1st Edition 2002
2nd Edition 2006
ISBN 1 – 9207711 – 00 - 7
978 1 920 711 009

Copyright © by Mel Hayde, (B.Ed., Sydney University)

All rights reserved. No portion of this publication may be reproduced, stored in a retrieval system or transmitted in any form, by any means – electronic, mechanical, photocopy, recorded or otherwise – without prior permission of the publisher.

Published by Terrific Toddlers, Sydney, Australia
www.terrifictoddlers.com.au
info@terrifictoddlers.com.au

Growing Families Australia
www.gfi.org.au
enquiries@gfi.org.au

BabyWise Bliss
www.babywisebliss.com.au
info@babywisebliss.com.au

Cover designed by Dawson Graphics
dawsongraphics@iprimus.com.au
0403 990 251

Printed in Australia by The Dominion Group, Sydney, Australia
www.thedominiongroup.com.au
admin@thedominiongroup.com.au

Introduction

Hi! I'm Mel, and this is the first book I have ever written. As you will no doubt notice, I'm not a writer as such. However, I just love toddlers, and as a mum I have a great passion to share some thoughts with you that may help you enjoy your toddlers, not just endure them!

So, who am I? I'm an Australian married to a Kiwi called Kris. We have three children, Caleb (13) who loves soccer and guitar, Emily (11) who learns ballet and clarinet and Sam (8) who enjoys tennis and keyboard. I love my children and have greatly enjoyed these early stages of my parenting. I have also had the privilege of counseling many, many mums almost daily, for over ten years.

The basic message of the book is this –

"As parents, you can influence your child's behaviour, character and choices."

We are not just passively observing our children's behaviour; we can be pro-actively and positively influencing their thoughts and actions.

Isn't that great news!

You don't have to endure the typical "terrible two's" toddler.

Through these next few pages I'll present a plan that can assist you in creating a daily environment of peace and enjoyment for you and your toddler. The toddler years can be terrific!

Foreword

At a time when there is much negativity and uncertainty about parenting toddlers, Mel's book, 'Terrific Toddlers' is a refreshing drink of clear, cool water bringing refreshment, revitalization, confidence and hope to parents.

When we bring those precious little ones into the world we have such high hopes and aspirations for them. Somehow the dream gets a little tarnished along the way! It is in the toddler years that vital foundations are laid for the rest of our children's lives. Laying them well is vital. 'Terrific Toddlers' is a very practical, easy to read and implement guide to not only success, but joy and blessing, as you look forward to many happy years ahead.

Having known Mel and worked closely with her and Kris, over the past ten years, and having spent time with their precious children, it is with confidence and joy that we can recommend this, her first book. We believe it will be a blessing to every mum and dad who read it and determine in his or her hearts to practice the principles espoused.

Mel is a Contact Mum, and Mel and Kris were for some time our State Team Representatives for *Growing Families Australia* for New South Wales. They have worked joyfully and tirelessly for the Kingdom of God through the testimony of the family.

It is a joy and privilege to be able to commend to you, 'Terrific Toddlers'.

Bill and Joan Grosser National Directors, Growing Families Australia

Dedication

To
Kristopher,
Caleb, Emily, and
Samuel
My precious family

To Jo,
Your friendship,
And your wisdom
Is greatly treasured

To Andrew,
Your belief in me,
And your friendship
Is remembered always

Contents

1. A Picture Story 1
2. Positvie Parenting 5
3. Managing Anger 9
4. Some Basics 13
5. The Root Cause 17
6. Advantages 21
7. Balancing Act 25
8. Flexibility 29
9. Toddler Activities – part one 33
10. Toddler Activities – part two 45
11. Other Activities 61
12. Motivating Behaviour 63
13. Implementation 67
14. More Than One 75
15. Questions 79
16. Dad to Dad (by Kris Hayde) 99

Terrific Toddlers

1
A Picture Story

You have been very, very pleased. About 18 months ago you moved into a brand new house. Everything was beautiful, fresh and modern. You have greatly enjoyed every aspect of your new house and feel very comfortable there. Of course, there has been the odd little thing that has needed attention, but generally everything has been working fine.

Just recently however, you have noticed a few wet, sticky, smelly brown patches appearing on the pristine white carpet of your lounge room floor. A month or two ago you had just one or two a day and you were able to clean them up fairly well. However, now they are regularly appearing 10 - 20 times a day.

They seem to be wetter, stickier, smellier and 'browner'. Cleaning them is taking up a lot of your time, and you are feeling quite frustrated by this. You are also a little embarrassed. When friends come to visit, they can't help but notice your floor.

Luckily, three people come to your door, offering to help you with this problem.

The first man tells you not to worry about them, every one has them, just endure them and they will eventually go away. He also tells you they will probably reappear when the house is about 13 years old and stay for 5 - 6 years before finally disappearing for good.

The second man tells you that every one has them, and yes, they are embarrassing, but he shows you how to clean them up each time they appear. Yes, that takes up a lot of your day and it isn't very pleasant, but the patches are removed for a few hours and the lounge room looks fairly tidy, temporarily.

The third man tells you that you don't have to have wet, sticky, smelly brown patches in your house at all. He will show you how to work on the causes of this problem and how to clean the patches up so that they won't reappear.

He can also show you how not to encounter them in your next house. The only catch is that your current lounge room will actually look worse for a week or two, before the patches are removed for good.

Which man's advice will you follow?

The wet, sticky, smelly brown patches on this carpet can be likened to the problem behaviours that generally emerge in children around 18 months of age and last for two years or more.

Some books will tell you just to endure these behaviours, other books will tell you how to react to each problem as it appears.

My hope is that this book will help you understand the root of these problems so that you can be a positive, pro-active parent and avoid most of these unpleasant behaviours altogether.

Do you want a busy, happy, contented toddler?

Do you want to be a happy, positive, calm parent?

Terrific Toddlers

Do you want to enjoy your day with your toddler (or two)?

Do you want to be proud of your toddler?

YES?

Then read on!

Terrific Toddlers

2
Positive Parenting

Let's start by looking at being positive in our parenting. As parents we quite naturally work toward suppressing the annoying, irritating and sometimes embarrassing traits we see developing in our child.

However, by focusing on the positive, mums can enjoy the training process and your child will thrive in that environment too.

I estimate that about 90% of my training is positive and encouraging, with only 10% being negative and corrective. I have always tried to say three positive comments to every negative one, and that is quite difficult on some days!

Remember that you have eighteen years of parenting and so you can afford to work on one or two behaviours at a time, you don't need to achieve it all today.

Make your first contact in the morning special. A hug, or a snuggle in bed with mum and dad, or a simple 'I love you' sets a lovely tone for the day.

Always speak politely and kindly to your child, as so much of how your child will interact with their siblings and others depends on your model.

Terrific Toddlers

Speak with a happy and excited voice about the plan for the day or the new event. Children will usually follow our lead, eventually.

Praise your child for making good choices, particularly after a time of testing. As a 15 month old Emily was quite determined to touch the video recorder and we had to teach her that she could not. At times you could actually 'see' her little mind work as she would walk towards the video, put her little hand out and then bring it back in, turn around and find her toys! We would go overboard with the praise at this point, with lots of clapping and cheering, and more and more often she would choose to play with her own toys rather than the video player as a result of the positive reaction she received.

Praise them –

When they are playing with toys (not 'off limits' things),

When they share a toy with another child,

When they ask for a drink in a happy voice,

When they say hello politely to a visitor,

When they have their hair washed without screaming,

Whenever they show self-control –

Always heap on the praise.

Children love it and they need it.

Present your instructions in a positive rather than negative light.

For example, replace 'don't hit' with 'be kind'.

Terrific Toddlers

If you have more than one child you can direct a positive comment to one, rather than a negative comment to the other.

For example, at the table I will compliment the child who has remembered to sit still with their hands in their laps on their beautiful manners, and 99% of the time the other (who has not) follows.

I love being home with my children and we have made up lots of fun rhymes and songs that say 'I love you' (I won't embarrass myself by sharing those with you!).

Focus on teaching your child all the positive attributes you desire to see in their little hearts. Virtues of kindness, honesty, compassion, love, gentleness, patience, integrity, perseverance, hospitality, politeness, goodness, friendship, and cheerfulness are all a delight to teach to your child.

Write a list and then creatively teach them into your day. As you bake together, talk about sharing the muffins with others. As you work on a chore together, talk about doing it for the rest of the family with a cheerful heart.

Read stories displaying positive virtues, colour-in pictures of children sharing, display gentleness when cleaning and feeding the family pet, make up games and stories filled with fun and wise words.

Incorporate positive teaching into all your everyday activities.

This is fun and challenging for you and gives great significance to those cyclic tasks you have each day. It also ensures your toddler is receiving mostly positive words and instructions in their day too.

As a mum you set the tone for the whole household. If your

Terrific Toddlers

entire day were recorded on tape, would it be characterized by negative or positive comments?

Is your home peaceful and fun?

Do you enjoy being there?

Do your children?

3
Managing Anger

One rainy morning I had one child spill their whole bowl of cereal over the table and another child knock their glass of milk so that it shattered over the floor. I also had two loads of washing left over from the day before, a very grumpy school aged boy, and a toddler who had woken up and decided that today was a 'no' day.

Do you ever have mornings similar to that?

Many of the mums I have spoken to admit to struggling with frustration that leads to yelling, hitting and even verbal abuse. Some situations seem to test our patience beyond our limits. The depth of feeling a stubborn toddler can arouse is quite startling.

The following suggestions may help you minimize these outbursts.

Having a **flexible** routine for your day is the greatest tool to help you avoid many, many situations that are typically frustrating during the toddler years. You will be able to manage your responsibilities and your toddler in a calm and orderly way that will greatly reduce outbursts from you and your toddler.

Look after yourself in terms of nutrition, water intake, exercise and adequate sleep. During the Grand Slam tennis events I

Terrific Toddlers

stay up too late and I am a very grumpy mummy for those two weeks!

Plan some fun for yourself each day. I love my hour of reading or cross-stitch every afternoon and feel more relaxed afterwards.

Have a hobby or interest outside the children. A craft, sport, or just anything you can look forward to each week. Try and have something that 'grows' each week (for example a craft project) or something that has measurable progress or results. It is a good balance to the cyclic tasks we are responsible for day after day.

Ensure you have time away from being a mum each week. In the early years of my parenting I would meet with friends for breakfast every Saturday while Kris had the children. Yes, he dressed them in odd combinations (I would call them my rainbow babies!) and sometimes the housework was still there when I got back, but the break always lifted my spirits.

When speaking to your child, make sure you have full eye contact to save the frustration of having to repeat your instructions. This is particularly important for boys ... big and small!

Respond with proper instruction, the first time your child whines, and not the tenth. Your internal temperature will rise with every repeat.

Attempt to admonish your child in the same place, making an effort to discuss the behaviour in private, never in front of siblings or visitors. This helps prevent the parent from lashing out on the spot.

Leave your child in their cot or on their bed until you are calm enough to deal with the behaviour. I had one memorable

Terrific Toddlers

afternoon where all three needed to be dealt with. I put the older two on a bed each, the toddler in his cot, and sat outside with a diet coke! Fifteen minutes later I was able to go in and calmly deal with them in turn.

Try whispering when you are really mad, it can calm the situation.

Talk through situations in times of non-conflict. For example, have your toddler practice packing up their toys quickly when you are not racing out the door. Turn it into a fun game.

As you calmly and consistently respond to your child and the events of your day, your child will also follow your example and this will result in a peaceful home for you all.

Terrific Toddlers

4
Some Basics

First, let's just quickly highlight four obvious causes of toddler 'messes', or inappropriate behaviour.

DIET

Do ensure your toddler is eating healthy meals at regular times. Snack foods, take-away foods, sweets and soft drinks will all have a negative effect on your child's behaviour. Watch the amount of colourings and preservatives your child is consuming, and keep processed foods to a minimum. Make a written note each time your child 'explodes' and see if you can see a connection with food.

Regular behaviour 'explosions' after parties or food treats from visitors may be an indication that your child is sensitive to particular foods.

Keep take-away food for a rare treat, not a weekly expectation. Have three meals a day and fruit for morning and afternoon teas. Avoid snacking, or grazing all day.

Not sure if food is an issue? Try a totally healthy diet for six weeks and observe the differences in your child!

Terrific Toddlers

SLEEP

Toddlers need somewhere between 10 – 14 hours of sleep each day. Do ensure your child has a rest or nap each day and is in bed each night at a reasonable time. So many of the problem toddler questions are often the result of a tired child – too many activities each week (for the child and/or for mum) or irregular night sleep patterns. A well-rested toddler is much more likely to be a happy toddler.

TELEVISION

Evaluate your child's television viewing very carefully in terms of quantity and quality. Excessive television watching is detrimental to your child's physical, social and intellectual development.

Also analyse the content of the shows you choose for your child – are they teaching your child to be physically or verbally aggressive? Or do they model and promote kindness and politeness? Two 20 – 30 minute segments is a suggested guide for the toddler age group.

CLUTTER

Avoid noise and object clutter in your house. It is very important to ensure you have a reasonably quiet and tidy house to provide the best environment, in which your child can live and learn.

Clutter can create distractions and frustrations. It will also create bothersome delays for each of your activities in your day. Mum and toddler will be constantly frustrated if they need to search for crayons and paper or all the parts of a toy before they can begin playing. Have a place for each item and have an orderly system for storing all household objects, especially the toys. You can't organize mess – if you have too much 'stuff' then maybe consider throwing away or giving away the surplus to someone in need.

Excessive noise can also be distracting for your young child. Having a loud television on, a radio blaring and some music all playing in the house at the same time will hinder your toddler's ability to focus and concentrate. Have the television on for selected shows only and keep background music at a low volume.

A calm and orderly environment will particularly help your active toddler manage your instructions and his play tasks.

Terrific Toddlers

5
The Root Cause

What causes all the 'wet, sticky, smelly, brown patches' in the life of your toddler?

Basically they are the result of a lack of self-control.

A toddler will naturally be self-centred, selfish, generally loud, unable to amuse themselves for any length of time, demanding, prone to outbursts of anger, picky with their food, un-cooperative, destructive, unwilling to obey your instructions and unkind to others.

They are like this because they do not have control over their words, emotions and actions.

You can sit back and accept this natural state or you can be proactive and positive and train your child to be self-controlled.

A toddler can be others' focused, sharing, generally quiet, able to amuse themselves for 20 - 40 minutes at a time, compliant, not prone to outbursts of anger, great eaters, cooperative, careful, willing to obey your instructions and kind to others.

Which toddler would you prefer?

The following suggestions in this book will not give you a perfect toddler, but they will help you train your child in self-control and give you a plan not only to avoid many of the sticky messes, but also to create a harmonious, happy environment. It will also enable you to greatly enjoy the toddler years with your child.

So, how do you teach a toddler to have self-control?

You can train your child all day through their everyday activities of sleeping, eating, and playing, visiting, shopping and so on. Mostly it is done through play. This is fun for the child and positive for you.

By organizing your daily activities into a flexible routine you will be providing the ideal environment for your child to progressively learn to control his or her words, actions and emotions.

The walls of a house provide the structure of a home and must be in place before you start to decorate the interior of the home. If you tried to start decorating before the plastering and painting was finished, you would be quite frustrated, wouldn't you? However, once the walls are finished you can make your home beautiful and enjoy watching the transformation.

Likewise, your toddler will thrive in a **flexible** routine for their day. Once that routine is in place, you will be able to effectively teach all the positive virtues that derive from having self-control.

Parenthood involves much more than simply keeping your child dressed, fed and amused. Each activity during your day is an opportunity to develop skills on a number of levels. You will be teaching your child physical, social and academic skills appropriate for their age. Most importantly however, you can use each activity to develop self-control in your toddler.

For example, as your toddler does a puzzle he will be developing his fine motor skills as he learns to actually put the puzzle piece in the right hole. As you talk about the pictures in your puzzle you will be increasing his academic knowledge. As he learns to sit and complete the puzzle he is learning to focus and concentrate, hence indirectly developing self-control.

Or, as your toddler plays outside she will be developing her gross motor skills. As she plays in her sandbox she will learn about pouring, measuring, digging and building. As you teach her to play outside for a continuous period of time she will learn self-play adeptness and self-control.

Or, when you feed your child you are doing more than simply meeting his nutritional needs. You can also be teaching him manners and conversational skills over the meal. You will also be indirectly teaching him self-control as he learns to wait quietly for the meal and then sit still to eat it.

From your toddler's perspective, it is all fun play. From the parent's perspective it is a valuable teaching experience.

I don't really get very excited about preparing sandwiches for lunch day after day. But I do get excited over seeing my toddler able to sit quietly for the whole meal and to watch the progress of his growing politeness and conversation skills.

I don't particularly get excited over bathing my child every day. But I do get greatly excited over seeing my toddler develop the self-control to be able to sit and play quietly in the bath, and also remember the little rhymes or songs we sing during bath time every day.

Staying at home with my toddler is a privilege. It is also very challenging and has incredible rewards. Teaching your child to have self-control over his behaviours, attitudes and choices is one of the most precious gifts you can give him for life. It has great worth and is also eternally significant.

Working on the cause of toddler 'messes' is far more rewarding than simply reacting to them as they occur.

Hence you will have a happy toddler and a happy mum too.

I have seen many families turned from chaos into order and calm within a few weeks simply by organizing their day. You can do this too.

In the next few chapters I'll list the benefits of a routine for mum/dad and toddler. Then we'll look at the – what, why, when and how, of working out a weekly schedule that is right for you. Finally, I'll answer some of the common questions I have received relating to this whole topic.

6
Advantages

BENEFITS FOR MUM AND DAD

Having a **flexible** routine for the week is so very good for both parents, especially the main caregiver (usually mum). Here are some of the benefits parents most enjoy as a result of having a plan for their week. Do you want to have these benefits too? Can you add some more?

An hour, or more, to yourself each day. Hurrah!

A tidy house all through the day.

Don't have lots of toys to clean up each evening after the child has gone to bed.

Have a toddler, who regularly and happily picks up her own toys.

Balance between completing chores and playing with the child is obtained each day.

Have very few 'no's' in your day.

Be able to clean and cook without chaos reigning in the house.

Terrific Toddlers

Have time to be out with friends and still meet the responsibilities of home.

Have evenings free to spend time with spouse or friends as all tasks are completed during the day.

Feel calm and in control – most days!

Have a toddler who helps with the chores (great start for the future).

Be able to adequately manage the usually horrible late afternoon hours.

Have uninterrupted conversations on the phone and while visiting friends.

Have your own emotional, spiritual, social, intellectual and physical needs met over the course of a week.

Have fewer battles with your toddler each week.

Spend positive time with each child, every day.

Feel fulfilled at the end of each week, not frustrated.

Don't have a toddler nagging you to play or read when you are trying to get chores done, as there is a time for everything.

Have far fewer outbursts (times when you lose it) because all tasks are done in an orderly manner – most of the time.

A calm and orderly household for husband to arrive home to.

Be proud of your toddler and happy to be out and about with him.

Terrific Toddlers

BENEFITS FOR YOUR TODDLER

Having a flexible routine for your week is so very good for your toddler. Here are a few of the main benefits that many toddlers enjoy as a result of a planned week. Would you like your toddler to have these benefits too? Can you add some more?

Is generally happy and content.

Hear very few ' no's' in his day.

Is predominantly praised each day (great for emotional well being).

Enjoys a balance of play activities each day – quiet and noisy, indoor and outdoor.

Has the security of an orderly and calm environment.

Is free to be a child and simply play, not make unnecessary decisions all day.

Learns to concentrate for sustained periods of time and hence can greatly enjoy each toy fully.

Experiences true creativity and imaginative play.

Accepts and appreciates (over time) that mum and dad are in charge.

Does not need to constantly ask for things as knows there is a time for each activity.

Enjoys a balance between time just with mum, time just with dad, time to play alone and family time.

Feels esteemed as he practices tidiness and personal

responsibility each day.

\# Learns to be a valued and needed member of the family by contributing to chores.

\# Has her emotional, spiritual, intellectual, social and physical needs met each week.

\# Feels good because he is learning to do good.

\# Has a self-disciplined and productive lifestyle modeled to her every day.

\# Learns that other people are important too.

\# Experiences the joy that comes from reading.

\# Enjoys a wide variety of experiences at an earlier age due to his good behaviour, as mum and dad are happy to take him out.

\# Is enjoyed and esteemed by others.

7
Balancing Act

As you begin to plan your week, you must keep in mind the needs of each member of your family. Your **flexible** weekly schedule should enable you to meet the emotional, spiritual, social, intellectual and physical needs of each person.

EMOTIONAL – special times for two people to spend together to esteem, praise and encourage each other. This could be husband and wife, parent and child, or child and child.

SPIRITUAL – a quiet time each day for renewing and refreshing the soul and focusing on the eternal value of life. Also time spent teaching the child your spiritual values and holy teachings.

SOCIAL – a number of occasions each week for individuals to interact with those outside the family. 'Mums' need a chance to interact as 'ladies' as frequently as possible (i.e. to spend time outside their role as parent). Toddlers love to be out and experiencing a number of different situations.

INTELLECTUAL – Mums need to keep learning and reading either formally or informally and have other interests outside parenting. Toddlers need to be taught their numbers, letters, colours, shapes, animals, seasons and so on.

PHYSICAL – Time needs to be set aside every day for toddlers to run and play in an active way – some need an hour while others need three hours to burn up their boundless energy! Mums and dads also need time for exercise each week for their own health.

Wouldn't you love to have all of this in your week?

I know I feel happier and healthier when I have a balanced week.

Do you feel frustrated at times with the conflict of trying to: -

Constantly keep the house clean and tidy,
Cope with the daily piles of washing,
Creatively plan and prepare meals

AND

Spend quality time with your child in play,
Provide appropriate learning opportunities,
Simply have fun with your child

AND

Enjoy time out for yourself,
Pursue a relaxing hobby or craft,
Keep in touch with your friends and family???

Some amazing women can do all of this naturally, every week.

However, most of us need to plan it out.
A **flexible** routine will enable you to balance all these things.

Isn't that great?

It will take you between three days and three weeks to establish a **flexible** schedule into your family. It will be hard work during that initial phase. However, after that you will reap many rewards for all the years to come. The early effort is repaid many, many, many times over.

So do persevere. Every family will have a different routine, depending on the number and ages of children in the family, and the unique needs of each member.

One of my favourite quotes is this,

' If you keep on doing what you have been doing,
Then you will keep on getting what you have been getting.'

If you are enjoying being with your toddler each day and if you are personally enjoying a balance of activities and friendships, then you will probably continue doing what you are doing.

However, if you are not enjoying being with your toddler each day, and if you are frustrated by the lack of time for activities and friendships for yourself, then maybe it's time to think about whether to keep doing what you have been doing.

It makes sense to try something else, and therefore achieve a different result.

Convinced?

Let's get to it.

Terrific Toddlers

8
Flexibility

As you read through the following chapter, please keep in mind the importance of being **flexible**. This simply means being willing to adjust to the personalities and circumstances of your day. Your plan is meant to be a guide for your day, not the law.

The activities I have listed in the next chapter are simply suggestions. You may have a much simpler plan for your day, or it may be much tighter. Your day will suit you and your family.

Please note that you will have plenty of spontaneous moments with your toddler during each day. You are not marching through each activity in a regimented fashion. There is always time for hugs and kisses, and to listen to the new discoveries or stories your toddler loves to share with you. You will share the little sorrows and delights of your toddler's life within your basic plan for the day.

You may only be home three days a week, or you may be home five days a week. That will depend on your own social needs, the number of children you have and the stage your family is at.

The best place to train your child is in your own home. If you are out all day every day then you will be missing out on the best opportunities to train your child. However, staying home all day every day is not healthy for you, or your toddler. Find a sensible balance in the middle that works for you. Most mums I speak to aim to be home for three or four days each week.

My day does not always turn out like the day written out on the notice board in the kitchen. I often need to be **flexible.**

As the parent, you will determine the length of each activity. You may initially expect an activity to last for 10 to 15 minutes. Over the next few months you will slowly extend that time to 30 or 40 minutes for each activity. However, you will have days when you need to be **flexible**. You may extend the length of an activity if your child is really enjoying it. You may decrease the length of an activity if the child is struggling with it on a particular day.

If the child or yourself is ill, then you may both spend the whole day in front of the television or sitting on the lounge with a few books.

On a gorgeous sunny day you may choose to have most of your activities outside. On a very wet and cold day you will be doing most of your activities inside.

Phone calls and visitors are not interruptions to your day; they are a part of it. Graciously answer the phone or invite your caller in. Adjust your day to make them feel welcome.

If your toddler is uncharacteristically quite tired and grumpy, then simply give him an early nap or put him to bed earlier for the night. Sam's bedtime was usually 6:30 p.m. but there were many nights when he was grumpy and so was in bed by 5:30 p.m. or 6 p.m. Be **flexible.**

Also, be **flexible** over your whole week. You may usually be home three to five days each week and out for shopping, errands, visiting or child-based activities for two to four days each week.

If, however, you are working on a new behaviour then you may stay home a little more for a week or two. There may also be times when you need to be out every day for a week or too. That is all okay. Be **flexible**. Most weeks will be a balance of at home days and out days.

Flexibility is important as you respond to the different personalities of each of your children. One child may need far more physical activity than another child may. One may need extra times of quiet away from the busyness of the house. If one has a particular interest, then attempt to work that in too. One child may love books and another music, so do include extra time for those interests in your plan.

Every family is unique and you will pursue a plan that is best for your family. Think through the principles behind each part of the plan and decide if they will be helpful for you and your child. If you discover other activities that progressively build self-control into your toddler's life in a fun and pro-active way, please do share them with me. I would love to hear from you (my email address is on the front page).

Terrific Toddlers

9
Toddler Activities
– Part One

Well, time for the biggest part of the book – activities to put into your **flexible** routine!

I'll work through a sample routine here and give you an idea of what a day at home with your toddler may look like. As we go through I'll explain some of the reasons behind each activity and the benefits for mum, dad and toddler.

MORNING START

It is very important that you, as the parent, are in charge right from the very beginning of the day. It sets the tone for the whole day. Start your day at the time you choose.

Your toddler will probably gain a sibling or two over the next few years. Think ahead. If all your children learn to rise at the same time each day then you don't have the early birds depriving your sleepy ones of their much needed rest. That will help eliminate starting your day with a cranky toddler who really needed an extra hour of sleep.

Terrific Toddlers

Another benefit is that you will not rise to find that your toddler has been into the cupboards or bathroom, to make a huge mess to start off your day.

Since I am a night owl myself, it is so wonderful to know that my child will not be rising before 7:30 a.m. every day. If I were woken at 5 a.m. or 6 a.m. each day, I would be a very grumpy mummy - not a good start to the day for my child or myself!

Your toddler will be practicing self-control and patience as he learns to wait quietly in bed until his favourite song comes on. He is also learning to think of others – to be quiet so that every one else can get the sleep they need.

Isn't that great? To think your little one can be learning all of those things before your day has even started.

It will take a little effort to enforce this in your home, but it will be well worth the early work.

Use an alarm clock or favourite song to signal when the child is allowed out of bed.

Be very clear with your expectations. We expect our children to stay in bed and to be quiet before the alarm goes off. There is to be no talking, to themselves or to each other. They are allowed to read, but not play if they awake a little early.

If you have a very early riser (i.e. one who wakes up with the birds!), you may want to place a few books on the end of the bed for her to read until it is time to get out of bed.

If your child is currently waking, and getting out of bed, at 5:30 a.m. and you want your day to start at 7:30 a.m., then it will take a few weeks to get there. Set your alarm for 6 a.m. for a week, then 6:30 a.m. for the next week and so on, until you get to 7:30 a.m.

Terrific Toddlers

Sounds impossible? It will work if you have appropriate rewards for compliance and a suitable consequence for non-compliance. More on that later.

We start the day with lots of kisses and hugs and sometimes a family cuddle in our bed. Not only does that set a happy tone for the day but is also hopefully creating some special life long memories.

Note: We often move the alarm to 8 a.m. on the weekends – so Kris and I can have a sleep in! Little ones hardly ever notice the difference!

BREAKFAST

Before coming to the table, we expect each child to make their own beds. We do this right from the first day they are moved out of their cot to their big bed and they love to feel important. At first, they simply pull up their blankets, but by the time they are five years old, they should be able to do it fairly well. Gradually raise your standard and improvement will be evident. Keep it positive, praise their effort and ignore the lumps!

Have each child sit on their same chair each day at the table – you don't need to have an argument about who sits where, first thing in the morning. Just clearly and calmly state who is sitting where.

Remember your kitchen is not a restaurant - do not take orders.

You choose the cereal,

The topping for the cereal,

Terrific Toddlers

The small spoon or the big spoon,

The spread for the toast,

The way the toast is cut,

The type of drink,

Whether the drink is cold or warm,

The order in which the meal will be eaten,

The type of cup,

The type of plate, . . .

EVERYTHING.

Why is this so important?

As the parent, you don't mind if the toast is cut into squares or rectangles, do you?

As the parent, you don't mind if they have vegemite or peanut butter, do you?

Why?

These are very benign issues to us as adults.

From our perspective, it doesn't really matter how the toast is cut. From our perspective, it doesn't really matter if the spread is vegemite or peanut butter.

The important point here is who chooses if the toast is cut into squares or rectangles. Who chooses if the spread is peanut butter or vegemite.

Terrific Toddlers

If the child is making this choice, and hundreds and hundreds of other small insignificant choices all day every day, then he begins to feel as if he is in charge. So he will question your authority in a HUGE and HORRIBLE way at other times during the day (those messes on your white carpet).

I have found that as I made all the (seemingly) little decisions in my toddler's day, then I had very, very few big messes to deal with during those toddler years.

Think it through for yourself.

Does it make sense to you? Can you see how, from your toddler's perspective, he will feel like he is the boss if he is making decisions all day?

Of course, occasionally he gets to choose his favourite ice cream or a special video. From the age of three, you will also start to give him limited options (e.g. painting or drawing now?) so that he can learn how to make decisions for himself. By the time he is six or seven years of age you will find that he can make many good decisions for himself because you have firstly modeled appropriate decision making skills to him, and then gradually allowed him to make more and more of his own decisions.

Note: If you calmly decide to take away your toddler's choices, you will have an 'explosion' for three to five days, as they react to the change. After that, your days will be much calmer, and your toddler will be happier too.

At the end of breakfast, you may leave your younger child in the highchair while you do the dishes and clean the kitchen. A child can sit and watch or have one small book to read. You won't have a messy kitchen to clean up afterwards and won't have to try and get back to it later in the day. Most importantly though, your toddler is learning patience, slowly becoming aware that mum has work to do and is not just there to play with all day: he is building a little more self-control.

Or you may have your older toddler help you clean up. We start by having our little one bring her plastic plate or cup to the sink. Later you can teach her to wipe the table, wipe up some of the (unbreakable) dishes or sweep the floor. Don't under estimate what she can do. If you start small, do it every morning, give her lots of praise and keep it fun, you can have a four year old who can tidy the kitchen for you.

At the end of breakfast we read the bible and revise any scripture verses we have learned. As soon as our children can talk we have them learn parts of the Bible and read it every day. By starting early we hope it will simply become part of every day for their lifetime. This time is very short, often only a few minutes, and we have the Bible close to the table and the verses written out and pinned up in the kitchen so it is very easy to transition into this time.

ROOM PLAY

This is one of the best parts of the day for a toddler, and for mum. The child learns to play quietly for a whole hour by herself, in her own room.

The toddler is learning to play for a good length of time with just a few toys, and she is also learning to be creative and use her imagination with her toys. The child also learns to play in an orderly manner with her toys as she returns one toy to the shelf before playing with the next. Your toddler is also learning self-control as she stays in her room to play and doesn't keep wandering out. Most importantly, she comes to realize that mum has other things to do in her day, other than just play with her.

Terrific Toddlers

Mum can have a whole hour to have a shower, relax for a few minutes, put the washing out, mop the kitchen floor and get organized for the day. Each child has the peace and the space to play without being interrupted by their siblings, and you don't have any conflicts to deal with first thing in the morning. This time is great if you have one child – simply wonderful if you have two or more! Some mothers use room play just before dinner, so the children are quiet, not playing (or fighting) with their siblings and dinner can be prepared without interruptions.

Are you thinking, 'My active two year old could never learn to do this?'

Be encouraged, she can!

You will need to begin with a very small amount of time – maybe only 10 minutes for the first week. Clearly explain to her what you expect – for her to play in this room, with these toys. You choose the few toys for her. If you can have toys that are just for room play, this will greatly help you succeed here. Change the toys every few weeks to keep your child interested.

You will need to hover, just out of sight for the first week to ensure your child is safe and is not playing with other toys, drawers and so on. You will not get any time yourself for the first few days, but if you are calm and consistent, you will soon have an hour to yourself for years to come.

It is helpful to have something that clearly defines when this time ends, either a buzzing timer or the end of a special singing or story tape that the child enjoys. Give your child an abundance of praise for playing quietly and appropriately during this time. As your child happily plays for 10 minutes for a week, then you can gradually increase this room time over the next few weeks.

Have her pack up the toys with you. Do it in an orderly fashion, packing up the books first, and then packing up the trucks. This is showing her how to pack up and also the importance of taking responsibility for her own clean up, eventually! It also means you don't have an untidy room to come back to later.

If you need to do the final straightening of the room, have her sit on the bed to watch you, she will only be sitting for a brief moment, and she is practicing a little patience and not getting out of sight and into mischief.

If your child comes out of the room or tries to chat to you during this time, you need to have a calm and consistent consequence to motivate her to comply with you. More on that later.

Most mums love this idea and are very keen to have it occurring in their own home each day. Please note, if you try to implement this into a day that has no order and structure, then it will not be successful.

The self-control that you are teaching and modeling in your whole day is what is needed for each activity to be successful in your day. Also note that if your toddler is making lots of little decisions all day, then they will not be willing to obey you and stay in their room.

What if your child just sits in the room and won't play? That's fine, just keep working on increasing the room play time up to an hour and praise her for staying in her room during that time. She will eventually play.

If you do want to encourage her to play, then set a task for her to do at the beginning of room time, e.g. 'do this puzzle' or 'build a tower from these blocks', just to get her started.

Terrific Toddlers

FOCUS PLAY

This is my most favourite time of the whole day. This is when I focus solely on my toddler. It is a fun time and one characterized by lots of cuddles and affirmative words. The main aim is to build on my relationship with my child and fill up his little emotional tank so that he feels totally loved.

Some days we sit for 10 minutes, other days it's closer to 50 minutes. We read, play imaginative games, learn some academics, bake cookies or cakes, do craft projects together, work on puzzles together, colour-in, and so on.

The child loves this time and looks forward to it each day. I have always had focus play in the morning and I find that my toddler is then quite happy to play by himself for long periods for the rest of the day.

By planning to have this special time early in the day, I can then move through my cleaning and cooking without feeling guilty I'm not playing with my child, or feeling frustrated by the constant interruptions from a toddler who just wants a little attention. Hence mum and toddler are both happy!

Through the play activities during this time, I focus on positively teaching my child some attitudes or behaviours that we are working on at the moment. I will choose one thing to briefly teach each day.

For example, if you have noticed that your child is struggling to share his toys with his friends you may act out a little puppet show with your child that talks about why we share or how we share. Or you could find or draw some pictures showing some children sharing their toys nicely.

If you are working on teaching your child basic manners you could have a little tea party and practice your 'please' and 'thank you's' as you enjoy your water and sugar cups of tea. Or the dolls could act out being polite to each other as they play.

If you are working on helping your child not to whine you could have his trucks use a whiny voice and then a nice voice as they talk to each other. Positively talk about why we don't whine. Or you could have a number of small cookies and practice having a toy bear ask, in a nice voice, for a cookie (and getting one) and then asking in a whining voice (and not getting one).

The possibilities are endless.

Be creative and have fun with your child. Keep the teaching part to just a few minutes and ensure your tone is positive and encouraging. By training in this happy time, you greatly minimize the number of 'messes' you have in the rest of your day and you also greatly reduce the size of them too!

Rather than simply reacting when a 'mess' appears you can be proactively working to ensure they don't appear, or are very small if they do.

Always have your child help you pack up at the end of each activity so that your house is staying in order and you don't have to go back and tidy up later in your day. Your child can sit still just for a minute or two until you are ready to go on to the next activity in their day. All of these little moments of waiting during your day are helping your child build up his self-control and will greatly help his sustained attention skills at other times in your day.

Do you have more than one child? It is vitally important that each child has this focus play each day and it is possible to plan your day so they each have 10 – 20 minutes alone with mum. It involves some careful planning, and a little trial and error at first, but you can find a plan that works for your family.

Terrific Toddlers

You may have one child watching a video, playing outside or drawing while you have focus time with another. I know families with five children who even manage to do this.

OUTSIDE PLAY

All children need to run and play in the fresh air each day to get exercise and to learn gross motor skills. If you spend a little time ensuring your yard is safe, then children will be able to play outside by themselves for up to an hour each day. Obviously, you will listen and watch every few minutes to ensure their safety.

It takes a lot of self-control to play outside for the length of time that mum or dad has determined. Your child is also learning to be busy and active independently, and gradually understands that mum and dad have other things to do in their day for themselves and other members of the family too. During this time I complete my household chores for the morning, catch up on correspondence, emails and phone calls or, on my lazy days, I read a book or the newspaper!

Your toddler will naturally want to come in and out during this time, but with a little encouragement she will come to love playing outside for a solid block of time.

Another advantage of this is that you will not have sand, dirt or water tramped onto your floors all day, or flies and mosquitoes getting in through a constantly opening door.

Initially, you may encourage your child to be outside by herself for 10 – 20 minutes. You can start her off on an activity (for example, digging for a few minutes in the sand) or maybe provide a morning snack at the start of this time. When she is happily playing for this length of time then you can gradually increase it over the next few weeks.

Bikes, balls, climbing equipment and a sandbox are all ideal for this age group. For variety, we sometimes fill up small containers with water, blow bubbles, paint the fence with water, run through a sprinkler, use outdoor chalk on the paths, do nature craft activities, provide a large cardboard box (or boxes) for imaginative play or do some gardening. On other days we may visit a park or go for a walk around the nearby streets discovering 'treasures' or jumping in the rain puddles.

Toward the end of outside play I will often play with my toddler by catching, kicking, bouncing or rolling a ball, by playing cricket or T-ball, roller skating (on the Pre-school skates that barely roll), building roads or mountains in the sand, explore the garden and so on. Then we pack up together for all the reasons previously mentioned.

If you have a very active child then it is very important that he or she learn how to run and play outside for at least an hour each day. The child who has boundless energy needs a positive outlet for this or you may experience problems later in the day, particularly in the late afternoon. My Sam was extremely active and so he had at least two (very long!) outside play periods each day.

10
Toddlers Activities – Part Two

I hope you are beginning to appreciate all the benefits that derive from implementing a positive plan into each day. Mum and toddler are happy! I find it so exciting to be able to enjoy a productive and varied day with my toddler that is also fun.

Let's now look at what you may include in the rest of your day.

LUNCH

Lunch is not only a time to meet your toddler's nutritional needs.

It can also be a time to train your child in self-control. You can give your child a sandwich to eat as he wanders around the house. However, not only will you have crumbs and bits of food to clean up later, you have also missed an opportunity to train.

Have your child sit quietly at the table while you prepare lunch. Use a highchair or booster seat with a strap until he has enough self-control to sit on a big chair independently. It really only takes a couple of minutes to make a sandwich and cut up some fruit. Again, you make the decisions concerning every part of the meal. As you work you can go through the alphabet or nursery rhymes together. Give your child lots of praise for sitting quietly and patiently.

I focus on teaching table manners over lunch. It is the meal where I am best able to focus on this. Be patient and teach one rule of etiquette at a time. There are many table rules that your child needs to learn but you have plenty of time to teach each one. Be creative and have fun as you teach your child the how and why of table manners.

QUIET READING

From the time my children were six months old I have always had the reading time straight after lunch. I simply wipe clean the highchair or place mat and pop out two or three books to read. I can then clean the kitchen uninterrupted. I start with about 5 minutes of reading time and build up to 30 minutes over the next six months.

The child is learning to focus and concentrate, to love books and is also developing the self-control to sit and read what, when and where he is told. Mum may also sit and read during this time to model that reading is important and also for her own enjoyment. The skills gained during this time will transfer to doctor's waiting rooms, to watching older siblings at sporting events and to those long queues at the supermarket.

I also focus on having my toddler read quietly during this time.

Teaching your toddler to control his voice and words is an enormous task for parents. Having him practice not talking for just a few minutes every day will greatly pay off in other situations during your week. I simply say it is reading time with no talking now and read my own book. At the end of the time I simply praise him for reading and eventually he learn that it is a quiet reading time.

Emily, Samuel and Caleb all devour many books each week. It is so rewarding to see them enjoying and pursuing such a worthwhile activity. If you have a two or three year old then start with 5 minutes of reading time, keep it positive, give lots of praise and slowly build the time up.

AFTERNOON NAP OR REST

All my children had an afternoon rest every day until they went to school. I think it is important that little ones have a break from the busyness of the house, from their siblings and from mum. It also gives them a chance to practice some self-control by staying quiet and on their bed for an hour.

Caleb actually slept every afternoon until he was five years old, while Emily and Sam stopped sleeping in the afternoons at around three years of age. When they stopped sleeping, I would simply give them a few picture books to look at or a couple of soft toys for the hour, as they still needed to rest.

One mother, who had three boys in three years, had a compulsory rest time each afternoon as it gave everyone a break. As soon as the boys could watch a clock, she popped a clock into their room and said they could get up when the big hand reached a certain point. If they got off their bed before that point, their rest time was increased. Very effective!

I look forward to this time every day, particularly if we have had a busy morning. I plan something fun for me like cross-stitch, reading, exercise, and a long chat on the phone to a friend, quilting or simply resting. I have found this makes my days at home more satisfying and this hour also refreshes me to cope with the rest of the day.

If you have a **flexible** routine for your whole day, and you are making all the little decisions all day, your child will probably adjust to this expectation fairly quickly. You will also need to implement appropriate rewards for compliance and consequences for disobedience. More on that later.

WALK

Most days I get out of the house to go for a walk. I safely secure my toddler in the pram and walk as fast as I can for my own exercise. The fresh air is good for us both and it is a good break from the house (especially if we have had a difficult morning).

My own physical need for exercise is being met each day and my toddler is also enjoying a change of scenery and can observe the flowers, cars and animals we see along the way. While my toddler is also building a little more self-control by sitting in one place for the duration of the walk (getting out is simply not an option), a piece of fruit and a drink can also help pass this time.

You may decide to meet up with a friend and walk together each day, and chat as you walk. This makes it more enjoyable and knowing someone is waiting for you also increases the chances of actually getting out for a walk each day.

When Caleb and Emily were only small (baby and toddler ages) I would put them in a double stroller and walk up and down our hilly Auckland suburb for 45 minutes each day. It was such good exercise that I even entered a 10 km fun run and managed to finish the race. Having a goal to strive for motivated me to get out each day and it was also very satisfying to achieve my goal. Now I need a new challenge to strive for!

FREE PLAY

You may give your two or three year old a short time each day to choose where and how he plays. This time should be between 30 and 60 minutes in length. Maybe give him a broad choice between outside play, toys in the lounge room or play in their room. He can choose what activity to do in each spot.

How your child plays during this time will be a good indication of how his self-control is developing. If he plays quietly and happily in one place and packs up after himself then he has obtained a good deal of self-control. If he runs around aimlessly and gets into things he shouldn't, then you know you have some work to do.

If he copes well with this freedom, then you can extend the time or give him two periods each day of free play. If he didn't cope very well, and 'messes' characterize this period of time, then simply shorten it to 10 or 20 minutes each day and slowly build it up again.

Don't jump in too quickly. These times give you a chance to see how he is developing and help define what you need to work on.

One of my children coped very well from under two years, while another didn't cope at all until well after three years of age. I didn't despair; I just kept the rest of my day very tight, and made all the little decisions of the day until they slowly began to be characterized by more and more self-control. Now Caleb, Samuel and Emily generally make good choices and can productively organize their time each day after school and for whole days during the school holidays.

CHORES

From my observation, it seems that many very young children love to help mum and dad with the household and outside chores. Make the most of this early interest.

By doing daily chores a child learns that she is an important member of a team, and that everyone has a vital part to play in the running of the household. She will learn not to sit back and expect to have everything done for her. A child learns to be responsible for her own tidiness, and of course she is practicing self-control as she actually does her little jobs happily and promptly each day.

As a parent, one of my goals for my children is that they will be able to completely manage a household by the time they are fourteen or fifteen years of age. I am gradually training them to clean, plan, shop, cook, prepare and follow a budget, handle repairs, wash and organize an entire house. Not only do I want them to know how to do these things; I want them to have enough self-discipline to do these things each and every day in a cheerful manner.

So I begin when they are very young and we work on one thing at a time. For the first 1,000 days it is actually much slower to have a toddler helping you but the early training will pay off over the next 10,000 days so do persevere. You need to gradually raise the standard and be positive about all progress during this learning phase. Break each task into very small steps and be patient. This will be a very long process.

From about the time my child is one year old; I simply start by helping my child pack up the toys. Of course it is mostly me who actually picks the toys up for the first few months, but by being consistent and calm, my child eventually follows suit. Have containers for each type of toy to help make clean up easier for your child.

From around 18 months of age I have my child help me with the sorting and folding of the washing. At first he may just put each piece of clothing in the right pile. Then I will have him just fold the face cloths, then the shorts and so on, and slowly work away over the next few years until he can sort and fold every item of clothing. Having a five year old who can sort and put away the entire family washing is a great help.

Dusting, sweeping, wiping the table, wiping up (plastics only), raking or collecting leaves, getting the mail, putting out the rubbish, watering the plants, setting the table, baking cookies, putting soiled clothes in the washing basket, organizing toys into piles, stripping beds, washing vegetables, cleaning their bike, washing the car etc., are all tasks that toddlers are capable of doing – with supervision.

Keep it positive and praise his success. If you are patient he will eventually get to your standard. Do it with him and explain first. Always show your appreciation for his effort and his attitude. Give ownership to the tasks (for example, "Caleb and daddy keep our car washed and clean"). Redo any tasks discreetly and without ridiculing your toddler's efforts.

At age four, Sam learnt to wipe down the place mats after a meal. We did it every day and simply expected him to do his bit to contribute to the family. At first we focused on showing him how to wipe and how to put the cloth away tidily.

We praised him for being a good helper and while he was brushing his teeth I quickly wiped them again. He would never learn if we didn't let him practice or if we were negative toward his early effort. As it became his daily habit (doing it without prompting) we worked toward him actually cleaning the place mats adequately.

Doing chores together is actually one of the nicest times of the day for our children. We are all working together and they are being positively affirmed for their efforts and attitudes. I think their genuine contribution to the family also gives them a strong sense of belonging and feelings of importance. The repeated explanations and patience required in the initial stages are rewarded many times over.

TELEVISION AND VIDEO

A short time each day in front of a carefully selected television show or children's video has many advantages. By sitting still to concentrate solely on the program, and not just catching glimpses of a show as they wander around, your child is learning to focus and concentrate. Once again it is an opportunity to build a little more self-control into your toddler's life. Your child is also able to learn from and enjoy the program.

Don't allow the television to be on continuously. Excessive background noise is distracting both to your toddler's ability to concentrate on his play and also to his ability to hear and respond to your instructions. A quiet and orderly environment will greatly enhance your child's day.

Having your toddler happy and in one place enables mum or dad to get a few chores done in the late afternoon, like bringing the clothes in off the line, chopping some vegetables or squeezing in a quick phone call.

If you have a younger child you can pop him securely in his highchair in front of the television. Some mums give their child afternoon tea at this time to help stretch them out to the 20 or

Terrific Toddlers

30 minutes of the whole program.

For an older toddler, ensure you have him sit in a small chair or on a mat. Be very specific. You do not want him rolling or walking all over the lounge room. If he chooses not to sit and watch, then he simply sits on his bed for the duration of the program.

Sam tended to get hyperactive when he was tired and started to run around and get loud. Popping him in front of a show for a brief 20 or 30 minutes helped him get his body a little more under control.

We found the Character Building video series very appropriate for the toddler age group. Sitting and watching a little story on patience or kindness greatly helped our teaching of those virtues at other times of the day. Our two and three year olds just loved the little songs on these videos too, and hearing our little one singing about the importance of obedience or politeness was such a great joy. Unfortunately, this particular video series is no longer available, but I'm sure something similar will be.

BATH

I get many calls from mums asking me how can anyone manage to cook dinner, bath a toddler, feed a toddler, deal with a cranky toddler and their own tiredness, and eat and enjoy their own dinner. (Let alone be able to greet dad happily as he comes in from work!)

It is a difficult time of the day to manage. However it can run smoothly with a little practice. Your routine over the rest of the day will greatly influence the success of this phase of your day. If you are struggling with this hour or two, then tighten up your routine and ensure you are making all the little decisions through out the day for your toddler.

There are a number of ways to organize this time and I will share one plan with you.

I have always bathed my toddler around 4 p.m. in the afternoon. This avoids the rush and stress of trying to squeeze it in either just before dinner, when you are busy preparing the evening meal, or the time straight after dinner when your toddler is very tired and cranky, ready for bed and far less likely to be cooperative.

Make the most of the time when your toddler is in the bath. You can either make it a positive teaching time by practicing a kindness rhyme, a memory verse or an obedience song.

Or, depending on the layout of your bathroom, use the time to clean the bathroom. As long as your toddler is always in view you can use this time to clean your shower, sink and toilet without having your toddler underfoot. Safety must be ensured.

TABLE PLAY

While I am preparing dinner I have my toddler up at the dinner table seated in his highchair or strapped into his booster seat (depending on his age). My toddler is not touching things he shouldn't or getting dangerously underfoot in the kitchen.

He can clearly see me and we can chat as I cook and he plays. He is also not being bothered by, or bothering his siblings. My toddler is practicing self-control and I can quickly get dinner prepared and on the table without any 'messes' occurring throughout the house.

Terrific Toddlers

Choose simple activities that will amuse your toddler and that don't require any assistance or preparation from you. Some suggested activities include: -

Drawing on one piece of paper with a crayon, one or two cars or trucks to drive on the highchair tray or place mat, two or three plastic cups, a small chalk board and a piece of chalk, one doll, a couple of plastic animals to move about, magnetic letters, a few building blocks, a toy with lots of buttons, a container of pegs or similar to put in and out, a wooden puzzle, stacking cups or rings, dominoes, a 'Where's Wally' type book for young children, Fuzzy Felts, activity books, a mixing bowl and spoon to copy mummy, Playdoh, pegboard, or threading activities.

As you implement a routine into your week, you will find that your toddler can sit and play for increasingly longer periods of time.

Keep your meals simple during this initial stage so that your toddler will only be sitting for a very short period of time and you can encourage his effort through praise.

This time will change into homework time once your child is at school and the valuable skills learnt throughout the toddler and pre-school years will ensure a smooth transition. Each night I'm in the kitchen preparing dinner and answering questions, helping with spelling words or testing times table answers for my older two. Sam is also busily doing his own 'homework' or playing quietly at the table. It is a pleasant family time and very peaceful.

It is hard work initially to be preparing dinner and teaching your toddler to sit for table play at the same time, but if you keep it short and positive you will reap the benefits. On days where Caleb couldn't quite stretch out to dinner we would give him a small piece of fruit or a drink for the last few minutes.

DINNER

As much as possible we will try to sit down together as a family for dinner. Maybe once a week I'll feed the children early so Kris and I can enjoy a quiet meal and conversation just by ourselves. If I have had a very bad day then I'll move dinner forward and put everyone to bed early and enjoy a quiet meal after that. However most days we will eat together.

At dinner we focus on talking to each other and not on the food. As we eat, Kris and I have our own special talking time first. We catch up on each other's day, any interesting news or current affairs, and then I fill Kris in on the important events of the children's day.

This shows the children that we enjoy each other and have an important relationship as husband and wife, not just mum and dad. It also enables Kris to know what I have been focusing on that day, and whether the children need a quiet night with an early bedtime, or if they need some extra attention in a particular area.

As we talk, the children are eating their own meals and so we rarely have slow eaters to deal with. After five or ten minutes, we then include the whole family in the conversation. We ask each other questions about our day, affirm one another and have some laughs. We all stay at the table until everyone has finished eating.

Be very careful not to get into bad habits. You cannot make your child eat. Food can be a very powerful and emotive weapon for a toddler. Refusing to eat, or eating very slowly can evoke a very strong reaction in mum and dad and is very effective for gaining attention.

We give our children very small amounts of food and then praise them for trying it. They can always ask for more. We do not focus on what they are eating or the speed they are eating at. After a reasonable time we simply clear the plates without any comment on what was or was not eaten. Those who ate all their dinner receive dessert.

We don't coax or give second or tenth chances. Having the dessert in the middle of the table can be a very strong non-verbal incentive. This way dinner is peaceful and the child eventually learns that it pays to eat their dinner.

Sam, at two years of age, was eating one bean and two carrots with his meal (he had no trouble eating meat, pasta or potatoes). He had no afternoon tea so we were sure he had a good appetite for dinner. Most nights we have fruit for dessert. If he ate his vegetables he got dessert, if he didn't then he sat at the table and missed out. If he complained, he sat on his bed until dinner was over.

Emily is quite slim and has always had a very small appetite. She would only eat a few mouthfuls of food at each meal yet she was still happy and full of energy all day. She ate very little of a variety of foods. Caleb has always had a huge appetite and eats large platefuls of a variety of foods. So you can cater for your toddler's uniqueness, and still ensure they are getting adequate nutrition, without it dominating the evening meal.

This approach will only work if your child is characterized by self-control in other areas of their day. The other typical mealtime 'messes' of a toddler will also be minimized by an orderly day of structured play.

Once you have established a calm and orderly evening meal you can add some variety to your meal. Eat on an outside table or have an indoor picnic. Have a theme night with dress ups too. Go out for dessert, or eat dessert first.

On Sundays my children loved watching a family show while

eating cheese on toast on a picnic rug. Even as toddlers they could enjoy this treat because of their self-control. There are no spills for me to deal with as they sit still and watch. It is a lovely way to end the weekend.

FAMILY PLAY

Family play is simply a time when the family is together. The aim is just to enjoy each other and some fun activities. It is a chance to focus on the importance and uniqueness of your family. It can last 20 minutes or an hour, depending on the activity or the circumstances of the day. Be creative and choose things that each member of your family can participate in.

Watching a video together, reading a book out loud, playing a board game, charades, hide-n-seek, sock wrestling, tickles, looking through photo albums, talking about your own childhood, going for a walk, going out for ice cream, or playing with a favourite toy are a few suggestions. Or make up your own story with each person adding a line or two (with sound effects), toddlers love it and come up with some classic lines!

BEDTIME

Have a ritual for bed preparation. Do the same things in the same order at the same time every night. Each family will be different, just think through a routine that will fit for you. You may have a routine of teeth, drink, toilet, reading, talking with mum or dad, prayers and then lights out.

We have always asked our children if they would like to read their bibles for 10 minutes or have lights out. For some reason, they have always chosen to read. This quiets them down and also develops a habit that will last all through their lives. We also have the same peaceful music tape playing each night to signal that it is time for sleep.

With the lights out, Kris or I will chat for just a few minutes with each child about the day or any concerns they have – it is a positive time, we do not discuss any behaviour issues here. We end the day on a positive note with a quick prayer and then a hug and kiss goodnight.

If your child is currently going to bed at 9 p.m. or 10 p.m. then you may want to bring it back slowly. Aim for a 9:30 p.m. bedtime for a few days and then 9 p.m. for the next few days and so on. You will work back until you are somewhere between 6:30 p.m. and 8 p.m. for you toddler's bedtime.

As you work on self-control during your whole day, you will find that bedtime becomes very peaceful and predictable. You will then be able to enjoy time to yourself each evening to relax, chat with your spouse and friends, or pursue your own hobby. Your toddler will be well rested for the next day and you will be refreshed.

Terrific Toddlers

11
Other Activities

I have given you a sample day. You may implement some of these activities into your day, or choose some different ones.

Your day will look completely different to mine, because you are unique and so are your children!

Please note that there are many other activities you can implement into your day to teach your toddler self-control.

Poetry, science, gardening, cooking, craft, music, drama, arts, singing, prayer and bible reading, animal care and play, and computer play are a few more examples.

Many community-run programs are also helpful in adding variety and training opportunities into your week.

Examples include toddler gymnastics, music and movement classes, play groups, swimming lessons, dance classes, trampoline classes, choirs, MOPS (mothers of pre-schoolers), mobile pre-schools, weekly library story sessions, and so on.

The key is to choose only one or two at a time so as not to over commit you or your child!

Terrific Toddlers

RAINY DAYS

Do you struggle with being at home with your toddler on rainy days? I did initially. When it was sunny and fine I had lovely busy calm days with my two year old. When it rained we had chaos!

Over time I worked out a rainy day schedule that helped make these days enjoyable too. I basically follow my usual routine but I replace outside play and free play with some activities that we save for rainy days only.

My toddler will help me make a little paper bag lunch (one for bear too!) that we will wrap up and carry to our toy picnic on the playroom floor. Or we will make a little indoor cubby house out of old sheets for him to play in and eat his lunch in. I'll bring out the dress-up box or the craft box and we will have some imaginative play together. Another idea is to have your toddler safely in their highchair or booster seat and have them bake some cookies or muffins with you. You can give them a small piece of the dough to play with as you work.

To utilize some of that boundless energy try putting on a music video to dance around to, or playing some music tapes and marching around together as loudly as possible. Once or twice, at the end of a very long rainy week, we have put on our raincoats and boots and gone for a splashing puddle walk.

Another idea is to run a warm deep bath and pop some new toys in. I sit within view of the bath and write letters or browse through a magazine while they are having a long water play.

I'm sure you can think of other fun ideas for rainy days at home. You probably wont have quite as much time to yourself on these days, but if they have had a few active play times during the day then your toddler should sleep just as well so at least you will have your evenings to yourself as usual.

12
Motivating Behaviour

How do you think our children should respond to our requests and directions regarding their behaviour?

Well, personally I think they should reply, 'Oh mother dear, you are so wonderful. I greatly appreciate all the amazing sacrifices you make just for me. Out of my undying love and gratitude for you, of course I will obey you quickly and happily, this time and every time.'

Unfortunately, this is not reality.

Most young children do not respond to reasoning (for example, 'eat your beans because they are nutritious'), nor do they respond to 'no', or even a loud 'no'.

Toddlers respond to concrete consequences.

These consequences can be positive or negative. For example, a huge cheer and a hug for packing up the toys, or no dessert for not eating the vegetables, or a small treat for sitting on the potty all motivate behaviour.

If your consequences are calmly and consistently applied, then you will see positive changes.

Over time.

Terrific Toddlers

If you have a very stubborn child it is vitally important that you are (outwardly) calm when you are responding to their difficult behaviour. These children love getting an emotional outburst from mum and will often keep pushing until you explode. Consistently respond the first time to their behaviour and have a very firm consequence. Do not let them control the environment in the family.

Each of my children was born self-pleasing and lacking in self-control (though absolutely gorgeous too!) and all questioned and pushed the boundaries. However, one in particular was very stubborn.

This particular child took longer to achieve self-control in most parts of their day. This child also required much stronger positive and negative consequences for change to occur.

Our longest battle with this child, from around two years of age, was over squealing when bothered or frustrated. Many, many reminders to say 'no, thanks' or 'help, please' in those moments were given. Positive rewards were offered every time verbal self-control was shown. A calm, negative consequence was given every time verbal self-control was not shown. I was consistent.

We role-played and talked through scenarios in our focus play each morning. Our day was structured and I was making all the little decisions of the day. Over six months we went from 30 squeals an hour to about 3 a day. Some days were worse than others, and some weeks I felt we were going backwards. I did have times of despair. Things were, however, gradually improving and over time we saw results.

I share this story with you to encourage you. Some children are harder to parent than others. Some children do just love to be awkward and seem to almost enjoy 'bucking the system'. But do not lose heart; you can build positive virtues into all their little hearts, over time. Do remember it is often the difficult child that has the most delightful personality, so do persevere and enjoy the emergence of their special uniqueness.

Sometimes you will be working on a situation for only an hour or two, sometimes a couple of days, or maybe even for a few months. You will need to increase the intensity of the consequences over this time.

If you are dealing with the same issue over and over, then progressively increase the consequence. Maybe change your consequence, or combine it with another. The consequence needs to promote or deter a particular behaviour.

Also note that that each child will respond differently to various consequences. What worked with your first child probably will be ineffective for your second!

For example, what reason does an 18 month old child have for wearing a sun hat?

Parents will have cognitive reasons for expecting this behaviour. However, explaining the damaging effects of the sun's rays on the skin to an 18 month old child will not be effective. An appropriate concrete consequence, that is calmly and consistently applied, will be motivating. One child may respond to a light squeeze on the hand every time the hat is pulled at, while another child will respond to verbal praise.

Think through situations from your toddler's viewpoint.

Why would they obey?

Terrific Toddlers

13
Implementation

So, how do you implement a **flexible** routine into your day?

Find a time when you can have an hour or two without your child. Either at home when your toddler is asleep or when you can pop out to a café for a short while (with a baby sitter for your child of course!).

It is very important to have your spouse's input in this process. You may design a weekly plan together from scratch, or maybe one spouse drafts a plan and then discusses and 'fine tunes' it with the other. Either way, agreement between husband and wife is vital. Even though one parent is usually the main caregiver, the practical and emotional support of the other parent cannot be under valued.

Have a notebook or some large pieces of paper, a pencil and an eraser with you. It will take a little trail and error to find a plan that will work for you.

Write out the hours in a day down one side of the page. Draw a vertical line down the centre of the page. On the right side you will write out your schedule and on the left you will write out your toddler's schedule.

Put in your meal and morning/afternoon tea times first, then sleep or rest times.

Terrific Toddlers

Put in the blocks of time you need to do household chores. I'm not a great housekeeper so I tend to get everything done as quickly as I can in three blocks; you may need more or less.

From here, you have two choices. You can either plan to balance the rest of your day with a mixture of quiet and busy activities. Or you can work through each of the needs for you and your toddler (physical, emotional, social, spiritual and intellectual) and plan fun activities that will meet each of those needs.

You do not want to neglect your child all day, nor do you want her demanding your attention all day. Find a healthy balance between these two extremes.

Plan: -

Activities that are done with you (for example, an educational time),

Activities that are done near you (for example, table play while you are completing some chores) and

Activities that are done without you (for example, room play or outside play). This balance is especially important when you have more than one child.

Be sure to take your child's individuality into account. Is she happier in the morning or the afternoon? Is she active or fairly sedate? Does she enjoy craft or music? Is she an indoor or outdoor person? Is she very social or does she prefer to play alone?

You will not totally cater to your child's preferences, but you will lean towards them. For example, all children should be exposed to books from an early age, but your child may be particularly attracted to books, so may have two or three different reading opportunities each day. She could have a time to read alone, a time of being read to by mum, an audio story to listen to or a computer story to watch each day.

Aim for most activities to last 30 minutes. A few will be planned for 15 minutes and others (for example outside play) may last an hour. Remember that you determine the length of each activity, not your child.

Try to gradually increase the length of each activity as your child develops more and more self-control. Your two year old may be able to focus for 20 or 30 minutes on one activity, whereas your three year old may be able to sit and concentrate for 40 or 50 minutes.

Write out your routine, pin it in a prominent place in your house and try it out. Be positive and excited about each activity and have small treats for your child as they comply. Expect them to enjoy this new day, and focus on the fun aspect of each activity. Praise all the good you see and try and ignore the not so good (just for these first few days).

Draw pictures on your chart to describe each activity. Your toddler can help you do this. This gives you and your child a visual reminder of the order of your day. Most toddlers love looking at the pictures they have drawn on the chart and working out what the next activity for the day will be.

Put all but your essential chores on hold for a few days. Plan quick and easy meals for dinner. Be available to hover around each activity to encourage and motivate your child.

Evaluate at the end of each day. What parts flowed well? What part was a total disaster? What improvements have you seen since yesterday? Should you change any parts or give it a few more days to settle down?

Terrific Toddlers

Focus on the positive. If your daughter played in her room by herself for 20 minutes – praise her. You may have been hoping for 30 minutes, but 20 minutes is still very good for a first day. Remember it will take between three days and three weeks for you to see a total change in your household.

If at all possible, enlist the help of your spouse or friend to catch up on chores in the evening or to allow you to get out for an hour or two. It will be hard work during these first few days of change.

What do you do if you are working towards 30 minutes of reading time after lunch and your child will only read for 10 minutes? Praise them for reading so quietly and then simply read to them for the last part. At least they will still be sitting and you can gradually increase their quiet reading time over the next few weeks.

What do you do if your child wants to come in half way through outside play? Go and play outside with her. Tomorrow you can stretch her out a few extra minutes and within a very short time you will be enjoying an hour to yourself and your toddler will have also learnt to enjoy herself outside fully for that time too.

Some mums may think about implementing one new activity at a time into their toddler's day. This is not very successful for mum or toddler. Thirty minutes of structure and self-control training in the morning will be greatly overshadowed by a whole day of choices and freedom.

I would suggest you aim to implement structure into your whole day from the beginning. Although very hard work for the first week, you will see a huge change relatively quickly.

This is because it is the environment of orderly calm that is so helpful in teaching self-control, and each activity will help the next activity. The self-control it takes to sit and do a puzzle will aid your teaching of sitting and focusing during table play later in the day, or eating quietly at the dinner table.

Reread the advantages for mum and toddler of a flexible routine each morning and night during this first week (chapter six). Keep fresh in your mind what you are working toward. Be excited. You are working on the cause of toddler 'messes' and not just the symptoms.

Terrific Toddlers

Outlined here are two sample days for a mum with one toddler.

Breakfast	
Television	shower, washing, bathroom
Focus Play	
Outside Play	cleaning, tidying, extra jobs
Lunch	
Sleep/Rest	craft, read, relax, hobby
Free Play	
Table Play	
Outside Play	washing, phone, extra jobs
Room Play	dinner prep
Dinner	
Bath	
Family Play	
Bed	craft, read, relax, hobby

* *

Breakfast	
Room Play	shower, washing, bathroom
Focus play and Puzzle Time	
Outside play	cleaning, tidying, extra jobs
Lunch and Quiet Reading	
Sleep/Rest	craft, read, relax, hobby
Walk and Free Play	
Chores	
Television	washing, phone, extra jobs
Bath	
Table Play	dinner prep
Dinner	
Family Play	
Bed	craft, read, relax, hobby

Terrific Toddlers

A whole week may look like this: -

SUNDAY — Family and friends day

MONDAY — Day at home

TUESDAY — Mums' group or Play group

WEDNESDAY — Day at home

THURSDAY — Kindy gym or Tiny Tots Music class
— Friend over for lunch

FRIDAY — Day at home

SATURDAY — Shopping
— Visiting Friends

Terrific Toddlers

14
More Than One

It is possible to have a calm and orderly day when you have more than one child. Whether you have two children or five, from toddler age and up, or a toddler and a newborn, you can work toward a balanced week that helps meet the needs of every member of your family.

You will be able to avoid many of the toddler 'messes' and care for a baby, if your baby is on a **flexible** feeding routine. The DVD Babywise Bliss, which is based on the Babywise book, provides excellent practical advice regarding the care and nurture of your newborn.

If you do have a baby and a toddler, you will need to write out your baby's feeding routine first. Then write your own plan for your chores and needs, followed by the schedule for your toddler's day. Try and have this new routine in place a month or two before your baby actually arrives. This gives you a chance to iron out this new routine out and ensure you have regular 30 - minute times to feed your baby throughout the day. It also means that your toddler's day will be almost uninterrupted on baby's arrival. This will greatly help your toddler to accept the new addition.

Be **flexible**, and adjust your routine to meet the changing needs of your baby as he or she grows. In that first year of having a two year old and a baby, My schedule seemed to change every six weeks or so. I was constantly changing it as my baby had longer periods between feeds and changed nap times.

If you have three or more children, you simply will not be able to have an individual schedule for each child. You will need to do almost everything together.

The children will all have table play at the same time – the little ones will have small toys, the older ones may have a craft to do. For TV time, you may have the use of two sets to show age appropriate videos at the same time, or have an older child use the computer then. During outside play the older ones may have the freedom to play out the front of your house (depending on safety, of course) while the younger ones are playing in the backyard.

You may find that a weekly plan works best for you. Rather than trying to fit every activity into each day, you may plan to have some activities only two or three times over a week. For example, you may divide focus play time into craft one day, baking the next, singing one day and pre-school academics on the other two days. This can be a lot easier than trying to bake, sing and teach each day!

The greatest challenge will be working out how to have focus play with each child. The day sleep times or earlier bedtime of the younger child can be a good chance to focus on an older one. Taking one child on an errand with you and stopping for a snack and a chat is another idea (if your spouse, friend or relative is minding the other child/ren, of course!).

One creative mother of four would have a rotating hour in her day. Each child would have 15 minutes with mum, 15 minutes on the computer, 15 minutes doing puzzles and 15 minutes of play in the family room. They would then all have morning tea together and spend the rest of the morning playing outside.

Terrific Toddlers

Stay positive and keep implementing a daily schedule until you find one that works for you. Talk with other families who are also planning their week to provide an optimal environment for their family. Share ideas with each other.

I am constantly improving my day, sometimes in response to the changing needs of my children, sometimes in response to our current family situation, and sometimes just for a bit of variety.

Plan a day that your children enjoy, and that you enjoy too.

Terrific Toddlers

15 Questions

1. I am the mother of a 2 year old boy and a 4 year old girl. Every day is chaotic, noisy and messy. I'm exhausted and I am not enjoying them. I feel they have so much that needs working on. Is it too late to start training them? Where do I start?

Firstly, please be assured that it is not too late to start. It will be hard work, but it will be much easier to start today, than it will be to start in 12 months time. I often tell myself that it must be easier to work with the toys and tantrums of a 2 year old child, than it is the toys and tantrums of a teen!

Start with establishing a **flexible** routine for your day. Write it out and put it up where you can refer to it easily. The first few days will be hard but you should be noticing improvements by the end of the first week.

Once your days are relatively organized, start working on just one behaviour at a time. Don't frustrate your child, or yourself, by trying to change too many things at once. I usually target obedience first because that overlaps to almost every other problem area. If you calmly and consistently work on one frustration at a time, you will see progress, over time.

Don't forget to look after yourself too. Make sure you give yourself breaks each day, and have some fun times planned each week, just for you.

2. I have spent the last three days trying to organize my day into a routine. It is not working. My toddler seems more defiant and I'm exhausted. I am ready to give up.

Implementing a **flexible** routine into your day will be hard work. Your toddler will seem worse at first. It will take between 3 days and 3 weeks for you to see the fruit of this change. Maybe even a little longer.

Ensure you have a positive tone and over praise your child for everything during this initial stage. Put all but the essential household chores on hold. Plan to stay home for 3 – 5 days to get your routine established. Have very quick and simple meals planned.

Enlist the support of your spouse or a friend and try and get out for an hour or two these first few evenings.

Evaluate your responses – are your rewards and consequences sufficiently motivating your child's behaviour?

Re-read all the benefits of a routine (chapter six) for both yourself and your toddler. Those breaks during the day for yourself are well worth working for.

A happy and contented toddler will bring you much joy. Focus on the future. Success is just a few weeks away.

3. I was embarrassed today when my 18 month old child screamed for 10 minutes in the supermarket when I said no to some sweets. He was so loud. Can I prevent this happening next time? (This has happened on the last five shopping trips.)

Yes you can! As a mum you do greatly influence your child's behaviour. Within the framework of a **flexible** routine you can train your child to accept a 'no'. How? By calmly and consistently providing a consequence every time they scream their response. In the privacy of your own home, 5 - 15 minutes isolation may be an option for a child of this age.

Your child's behaviour in public is a reflection of what happens in the home, and as you train your child to have self-control each day at home, your shopping trips can become a pleasure to you both.

4. I am not a naturally positive person. I find it hard to find things to praise my children about. How can I improve in this area?

Thank you for your honest question. You may be surprised just how many mums struggle to be positive in the midst of their busy days.

Plan a short one-to-one time with each child. Regardless of what activity you do together (let the child choose, e.g. books or dolls) you plan on saying three positive things to your child. For example ' I love you', 'You are very special to me', or 'I'm so glad God gave you to our family'.

If they do something half right, then praise the good (you remembered to put your cup on the sink, well done!) and ignore the rest (the plate still on the table!).

Use mealtimes to share what each person likes about another family member. Start by saying one positive comment for every negative or corrective comment.

Then build up slowly until you are characterized by being three or four more times as positive. Your child will thrive on your praise.

5. I seem to manage okay with most of my day, but I'm finding that from after 5 p.m. each afternoon it's chaos. I yell at the kids and I always feel guilty afterwards, how can I stop this happening?

You firstly need to evaluate your schedule for the whole day. Ensure the morning and early afternoon is filled with a variety of activities that are fun for the child and are also instilling self-control.

Also make sure you get a little rest time early afternoon. If I have just half an hour to myself after lunch, then I'm usually refreshed enough to last to the end of the day – when I don't get that little break I'm inclined to get grumpy!

Then just experiment a little with your evening routine. A quiet video just before dinner, reading or a puzzle in separate rooms (particularly if they are prone to fight at this time of the day), drawing at the kitchen table are all options for when you are cooking dinner.

Try to bath either before dinner prep or after dinner is over to minimize your stress. Have the same ritual for bedtime each night (e.g. teeth, toilet, story, prayers, and lights out). Be encouraged, you can have calm and peaceful evenings!

6. My 17 month old daughter clings to me all day and it is driving me crazy as I'm not getting my chores done and I don't have a moment to myself! How can I get her to play by herself?

This is very common behaviour for a toddler, but you can work on this. Plan your day to include a balance between playing by herself, playing near mum and playing with mum. If you have the same routine for your 'at home' days then that will greatly help in training your child to learn that mummy is not there simply to entertain her all day.

Tips for getting chores done without a toddler underfoot:

Leave her in her high chair after meals with one book or one toy while you clean up the kitchen. Or pop her in the playpen while you iron or sort out a cupboard or put the shopping away.

Have her sit in her high chair to watch a short video or TV show while you get some cleaning done mid afternoon.

Clean the shower and toilet while she is in the bath (as long as you can still see her of course).

She can help you 'cook' dinner with a spoon and an empty small bowl while she's sitting at the bench or in her high chair.

To get time for yourself you need to work on training your child to concentrate and focus for long periods of time. To do this, you start with about 5 - 10 minutes per activity and gradually build it up to 30 - 40 minutes per activity by the time a child turns two. Room playtime, outside play, drawing, playing on a mat, and reading time, are all examples of activities you can use to teach this valuable skill.

7. I want my toddler to be able to play by himself at times and not to demand my attention all the day. He will not play outside by himself. How can I encourage this?

Ensure that he has outside play at the same time every day. Have some focused time together just before it is outside time. You may play outside with the child for the first five minutes then go inside.

Or you can try the direct approach of putting him outside and simply bringing him in after the 10 minutes is up.

When he learns to play happily for 10 minutes then you can increase it to 15, then 20 and so on. Begin outside play with morning tea, or start off with an activity to help the child get focused (e.g. 'Can you dig a deep hole in the sand?'). I always play with them at the end of this time and we pack up together too.

8. My 15 month old daughter has recently started to cry during her room playtime. We have been consistent every day and she is not ill or teething. What's happening?

It's probably due to one of two factors. Once children begin to walk they may temporarily not enjoy their room play because they want to be out exploring and practicing their new skill.

You may shorten room playtime for a little while but don't disregard it altogether, toddlers still need to focus and concentrate at times, and I'm sure you still need that break for your shower or to do a few chores.

It may also be due to your daughter's growing awareness of self and her expression of that. From this age you start to get the 'no' for many things and this may be one.

Calmly and consistently continue with room playtime and she should settle down in a few weeks. Ensure the toys are age appropriate and that there are only 3 – 4 toys in the room.

Playing the same music tape until its end or having a timer for the finish may help.

9. I love the idea of mat time. I can think of so many times where it would be useful to have my very active 3 year old boy sitting in the one place! How should I begin?

Ensure you have a **flexible** routine for your whole day. Choose a time in your day when your child is fresh and you are free to train.

Place a picnic blanket or similar on the floor and choose a small basket of toys. A wooden train set, building blocks or a car set are good choices for a boy of this age. Simply explain to your child that he needs to play here with these toys.

Be positive and expectant. Keep it very short, 5 minutes, and give lots and lots and lots of praise (or even a small reward like a jellybean) at the end. A timer can be helpful to let the child know that the clock and not his asking or whining determines when mat time is over.

You could try starting with a snack and then doing an activity that has a definite end (like an easy puzzle). If he sits but doesn't play, simply praise him for staying at the end of the 5 minutes. Ensure you have a physical activity planned straight after mat time so he can run around again. If you are calm and consistent every day, you will see progress, over time.

10. My 15 month old is constantly touching the stereo and I feel like I am saying 'no' all day. Please help.

Two things will help here. The first is a **flexible** routine for your day. Have a look at the suggestions in this book and adapt it to your needs. A toddler will only have one or two lots of free time each day so they can't even be near the stereo most of the day. Hence you will have a lot less 'no' in your day.

When your child does have free play, ensure you are available to train them. If you immediately isolate them for 5 - 10 minutes you will probably only have 2 or 3 'no's' for that time and then you move on to the next activity in your day.

If you have a routine for your day, and you have been consistently and calmly applying consequences for a particular behaviour, then you need to look at increasing your consequence. Try 10 - 20 minutes of isolation each time. Give lots of praise for playing with their toys and not touching the stereo.

11. My toddler and preschooler fight and annoy each other for most of the day. How can I have some peace in my day?

First organize your day into a **flexible** routine. You want to balance out the time your children spend together and apart.

This will help minimize your frustration and you can plan their times together for when you are free from chores and can proactively teach them how to share and how to resolve their little conflicts.

They can be apart during room time (if they share a room for sleeping simply have one of them use your room for this playtime).

One child can watch a short video while you have a fun focus time with the other child and then swap them over.

One child can do a quiet activity up at the table while one child has outside play. If they do have times apart each day then they are more likely to appreciate and enjoy the times they are together.

12. My day is fairly organized and so my three little ones are mostly happy and content. However they seem to fight a lot over outside toys. How do I teach them to share?

Do be aware that this is a process that will take some time. Ensure you are free during this activity of the day so you don't feel frustrated by any interruption.

When you hear the squeal, intervene straight away. Using a firm, quiet voice, talk them through the situation. I taught my children to say 'no thanks' rather than squeal. If the other child doesn't respond to that polite plea, then the child can come to an adult for assistance.

At first we aimed for them to simply take short turns with a toy and not to grab from the other. A timer can be very useful here initially. If one child refuses to cooperate, then they simply lose the freedom of playing with their friend, or that toy, or both, for that day.

13. I have always wanted my children to be best friends throughout their childhood and into adulthood. Is this just wishful thinking?

Definitely not! This is one of my most cherished parenting desires. Tell your children right from the beginning that they are best friends.

Encourage them to love each other through kind words, short notes, little gifts, hugs and kisses, little acts of service and interest in each other's activities. You can foster these precious relationships.

14. Thank you, so much, for all your advice on proactively training my toddler. I've now implemented a flexible routine into my day. I was skeptical at first but the changes have been amazing. We still have little battles over what to do during each activity (e.g. I'll choose the crayons and she'll want the pencils for drawing time). Can I minimize these?

I'm so pleased to hear that things have improved for you. Do remember that while a **flexible** routine will not prevent all your battles, it will provide an environment to help you pro-actively teach and train your children.

I suggest that you make all the decisions for your 2 year old. When she can generally accept your decisions, and then you can start to give her limited choices, for example the Wiggles or Hooley Dooley's video for TV time.

As the mum, you probably don't mind which video of the two she may choose, and feel quite ambivalent about the issue. However it is the decision making process and not the object of the choice that is crucial to your child. If she makes lots of decisions, she will feel that she is in charge, and will therefore constantly question your authority all day.

15. My three year old girl whines all day and I have tried everything to stop it. Can you offer me any suggestions?

First, have a medical check up to ensure there is no physical reason for this whining if it is excessive.

Ensure that you are implementing a predictable and balanced routine into your child's week. The vast majority of the whining will disappear when your child knows what is happening when.

For example, if you have morning tea after focus play every

day, then the child will not need to be asking for food all morning. If you always have a video straight after lunch, then she will not need to constantly ask to be watching one.

Then you need to evaluate why she is whining. Is she simply copying the people around her?

Some children whine in their requests for food or a video etc. Simply have her sit in a chair, set your timer for 2 or 3 minutes and then have the child ask again, nicely this time.

After a day, double the time she has to wait. I have seen some very determined whiners cured in just a week using this idea.

Your child may be whining to get attention. Ensure you have a focus time with each child every day, even 10 minutes with mum is effective.

Most children however will whine because they do not like your instruction and this is their way of expressing that. Treat it as if she had overtly rejected your authority and apply a strong consequence.

We found that 10 – 20 minutes of isolation for a whine response was most effective. Be calm and consistent, every time.

16. When I say 'no' to my 14 month old she just laughs at me and does it any way. If I smack her hand, she barely cries and still does what she chooses. I'm nervous she will hurt herself if she continues to touch dangerous things. How can I help her obey me?

Read back over chapter ten on what motivates a child to obey. A 14 month old is just starting to test the boundaries and this is very normal. 5 - 15 minutes of isolation can be quite effective for disobedience at this age. For her own safety, she needs to learn that a 'no' from mummy is often protecting her from danger. Also give lots and lots and lots of praise for compliance. Encouragement is a great motivation for us all.

17. Meal times are horrible with my two boys. They are loud, they fight and they will not sit still for the whole meal. I would like my mealtimes to be pleasant and filled with happy conversation. Should I just give up?

Mealtime behaviour is often a reflection of what is happening during the rest of the day. Tighten up your routine and make sure you are making all the decisions for your boys during the day.

They should only have only one or two free play times at this age. As you work on self-control, through play, each day, you will have more pleasant meal times.

Maybe leave your own meal to eat in peace later and be available to train. Work on one thing at a time.

For example, you may first work on teaching them to be quiet. Clearly state your expectation 'there will be no talking until you have finished your meal'.

Also clearly state the consequences for compliance or disobedience. Rewards may include a sticker on a chart (5 stickers for a small toy) or dessert (a healthy one of course). Isolation, no dessert or simply putting them to bed for the night (with a drink first) may motivate your boys to obey.

If you are calm and consistent, you will see changes.

18. My 4 year old will not initiate his toilet visits, and we are having 8 - 10 accidents a day. How can I encourage him to remember?

Simply have him sit on a chair after each accident. He sits, and doesn't play or talk for 5 minutes (use a timer). Try doubling this time every few days. Reward him for remembering, for example, five stickers then he gets a small toy. Be calm and very matter of fact. Calmly tell him that this is a skill that every one needs to learn.

You may go back to planning regular toilet visits into your day. For example, after lunch and reading time, you will instruct your son to go to the toilet, and then move onto rest time. After a few days you can ask your son to tell you what comes after reading time, and then gradually he can initiate the toilet visit at that time himself. Reward him for remembering.

Having a child helping to clean up after the accident is effective for some. Not only does he experience all the work and time that goes into the clean up process, he is also losing out on playtime – much quicker simply to go to the toilet!

19. I started toilet training my child at 18 months of age and nine months later she still has accidents every day. She can stay dry for at least an hour and always tells me after her pants are soiled! Help!

You have probably started a little too early, as you would want her to be regularly dry for 2 - 3 hours at a time before you start training. However, as you have started, do keep going.

Praise her for telling you when her pants are full and watch for her pattern. If, for example, she starts to always pass a motion after lunch then you can sit her on the potty and try to catch it.

Read a book to her or practice her counting or ABC's to make the most of the time! Pop her in thick toweling training pants to decrease accidents on the floor, and your frustration too!

Be calm, patient and consistent and she will catch on in the next few months.

20. We always seem to have a tantrum around 2 o'clock every afternoon. Why is this happening, and what can I do?

A tantrum at the same time each day can usually be related to a specific cause. In this case, as you are on one nap a day, it is probably mostly due to tiredness. Rearrange your schedule and pop your little one into bed half an hour earlier.

21. My little one is fairly obedient most of the time but about once a week we have a major explosion and he can be screaming for over an hour. How can I prevent these episodes?

Evaluate your routine to ensure your day is well balanced and structured. Are you too busy? Is your child too busy? Is this mostly a result of fatigue? Cut out a few activities (yours and his) for a week or two and see if that helps.

It may also be the result of too much free time. One or two periods of free play (say around 20 - 40 minutes each) every day are adequate for a toddler. Are you giving him too many choices? It is very easy to fall into the habit of asking our child to make countless decisions.

Outbursts like this are usually due to a build up of tensions or frustrations. So look for the warning signs. Some children may whine a little more before a major outburst, others may have a louder and angry tone, and others simply get more bouncy and over active. By intervening with a quiet cuddle and special reading time with mum, you may help prevent the outburst even starting.

22. I feel like I am saying 'no' all day. I don't enjoy it and it doesn't really seem to be effective. Is this normal?

Organising your day will help avoid many, many 'no's. Once you have a **flexible** routine, then look at using a variety of consequences to motivate your child's behaviour.

Remember to only focus on one major behaviour at a time. Please do not underestimate the power of praise and positive expectation. Reinforce good choices over and over again.

Here are a few ideas:

Isolate to the cot if they won't sit for TV

No dessert for not eating vegetables

Simply sit in high chair if toy is thrown to floor

Wash their hair, scream or no scream

Sit for reading time if they read or not

Stay outside for outside playtime if happy or whiny

Lights out if they play, rather than read, just before night sleep.

If you are calm and consistent with your consequences (positive and negative) you will see changes, over time.

23. I think it is appropriate to show my children when I am angry with them. When I yell and scream they certainly know that I am cross. Is this okay?

Two things to think about.

Firstly, do the actual words you use during your outburst ridicule or esteem your child?

It is very important to express our displeasure at our child's actions, and not them as a person. We love who they are, but we don't always love what they do.

Secondly, it is important to realize that our children listen far more to our actions than our words. We model to them how to cope with anger. They are watching and learning how we relate to our spouse, peers, and to them, especially in conflict situations.

Do we yell, scream and shout or do we calmly and rationally present our honest view?

They will model our behaviour back to us.

Think ahead, do you want a teenager who yells when angry or one who can calmly talk an issue through?

By the time Caleb was twelve years old, he, at times, strongly disagreed with a decision we had made for him. He had enough self-control to sit and discuss an issue with me. If things get a little tense, then he, or I, would suggest a little break for a few minutes until we were able to discuss it calmly again.

My heart is deeply touched by this and gives me great hope for the years ahead. I wish I had been able to deal with conflict in this way during my younger years.

24. My three year old will not stay in bed at night. We have a story and a long cuddle before I say goodnight, but she will be up within five minutes. This can go on and on for an hour or two each night. I would like, and really need, my evenings to be uninterrupted for myself.

First, examine if your daughter is going to bed at the right time. Too early and she will not be tired enough to sleep, too late and she will be overtired and will have difficulty putting herself to sleep. All toddlers are different, but somewhere between 6 p.m. and 8 p.m. seems to suit most.

A **flexible** routine for your day will provide the framework for you to proactively teach your daughter self-control. It is self-control that enables a toddler to stay in bed all night. As you work on her self-control all day every day through the fun play activities, your daughter will learn to stay in bed.

Also think through your response each time your daughter gets out of bed. You need to have a very calm consequence that is meaningful to your child. Reward her first thing in the morning if she has managed to stay in bed. Praise her good choice and be very positive.

25. I am saying 'no' every day to the same issues. For example, I have to remind my three year old daughter not to touch the flowers in my garden every time she is outside. It is all rather tedious. What can I do?

A 'no' does not motivate a child to change. Concrete positive and negative consequences motivate behaviour. Add some meaning to your instruction by following it up with a positive reward for compliance or a negative response for disobedience. If you are calm and consistent with the appropriate reaction, you will see a change.

Also note that your toddler is most capable of remembering from day to day. If you choose every morning to give your child four warnings before following through on a consequence, then you can be sure she will touch the flowers at least four times every day. Respond the first time each morning.

26. When I say 'no' to my 18 month old girl, she stops what she is doing but then goes straight to another 'no' situation. I will say 'stop playing with the phone', and she will, but then go straight to the video player. I will say 'stop playing with the video' and she will, but then goes to the drawers. It is a constant cycle until I can distract her or feed her.

Do ensure you have a **flexible** routine to your day. You want to minimize the amount of time your little one is able to simply roam around. This will be more pleasant for both of you.

Saying 'no' does not motivate your child to change. You need to give her a reason to obey. Toddlers will not respond to the reasoning of words. They will respond to concrete consequences. Lots of cuddles and kisses or small treats when she is not touching these things will be motivating. A quiet but firm no with 5 – 15 minutes of isolation in her cot would also be motivating.

27. I am really struggling with . . . . we have been working on this particular behaviour for months without seeing any improvement. I have been calm and consistent with my praise and consequences. It is driving me crazy. Please help.

If your toddler is going toe-to-toe with you on one issue, then you need to look at the big picture. It is normally an indication that your overall day is too loose for that particular child. You need to tighten up your routine. If your day has been divided into one-hour time slots, then tighten it up lo 30 - 40 minutes per activity. Watch the transition time between activities. Have your child sit and wait until you are both ready to move on; don't allow him 5 – 15 minutes of aimless wandering around.

Ensure you are making the hundreds of little decisions each day that relate to your child.

Are you expecting self-control in all areas of the day, or only in those areas that maybe embarrass or frustrate you?

Are you out more than you are at home? The best environment for training is in the home.

Are you and your husband parenting 'on the same page'? The efforts of the stay at home parent can be undermined, or greatly strengthened, by the attitude and support of the spouse.

If you are consistently teaching self-control in all areas of your day within the framework of a routine, if you are home most days and if you are making all the decisions for your toddler, then you have the right environment to work on this issue.

Gradually increase your positive and negative consequences when you deal with this behaviour. Apply them immediately, calmly and consistently.

Be patient.

You will have good days and bad days, but you should be seeing a gradual improvement from week to week. You will reap fruit if you diligently sow.

28. I love being a mother and I enjoy staying home with my children. My week is fairly balanced and I'm out three times a week, have friends over once or twice and try to have at least three or four days at home. I have time for my children, my husband, my friends and myself. It's great! Thank you.

Thank you for your most kind words.

It is an amazing privilege to share with you these few simple ideas and suggestions that I have found helpful myself, and to learn that they have been an encouragement to you also.

I pray that each of you may have a joyful, happy home, and that you will come to treasure and enjoy these precious years with your little blessings from heaven.

16
Dad to Dad by Kris Hayde

Hi Dad. If you're reading this book and made it to this chapter then you either love your kids enough to have a real interest in building moral character in their hearts, or perhaps things are not going well and you love your kids enough to look for some answers. More than likely it's a bit of both. Be assured there is no such thing as the perfect parent.

You will have observed those poor parents who experience Typhoon Toddler. You watched as Typhoon Toddler quickly lost control, leaving a wake of anger, frustration, despair, parental conflict, perhaps even actions one would later regret, not to mention the public humiliation.

You wondered to yourself 'what kind of a monster is that kid going to be when he/she becomes a teenager'. Secretly, you hoped they would not move Typhoon Toddler into your kid's school, or, worse still, move in next door and become your neighbours.

So, how do you want YOUR toddler to behave? Let me tell you what toddlers are capable of then you can decide. First up, don't ever accept the 'Oh, Junior is only 2' excuse for bad behaviour. When this excuse allows bad behaviour to go untrained you can be sure a future Typhoon Toddler is gathering momentum. Parenting is TRAINING.

A toddler can be trained to sleep through the night every night, eat food quietly and calmly without fuss, treat yours and other people's property with respect, and treat you and other people with respect. Toddlers can develop enough self-control to spend a good hour each day by themselves playing while Mum or Dad goes about their business.

They CAN understand the difference between good and bad choices and that each choice has appropriate consequences. Last, and certainly not least, toddlers CAN obey the first time an instruction/command is given.

Can you imagine the academic and social/relational benefits of these moral skills to your child? There's much more, and the list would take the rest of this chapter, but you get the point. Typhoon Toddler does NOT have to visit your home, if you really commit to moral heart training.

The big question is, are you prepared to do the hard yards for the better result or not? Parenting is not without its challenges and frustrations. It is hard work and requires some pain. But consider this, you will work hard and experience pain one-way or the other.

You can work hard cleaning up Typhoon Toddler's aftermath, wondering when the next episode will be and will it embarrass you in public. Or, you can work hard to build a child who grows in self-control, obedience and respect for others.

The good news is if you concentrate on building character in your child's heart you will experience far less pain and heartache, now and in the future. I know this for a fact! To me the choice is obvious. YOU WILL REAP WHAT YOU SOW. How much pain you experience is your choice, not Toddler's.

Terrific Toddlers

There's something else I know for a fact. The joys, blessings and victories you experience from consistent moral heart training are worth every ounce of the hard work. That's a massive understatement.

Therein lies the emphasis of this book. It explains some of the everyday, practical "how do you do it?" methods to build moral character in your child's heart to make the toddler years a blessing and a pleasure.

The ideas in this book really work.

My wife regularly gets letters, emails and phone calls from Mums explaining how things have changed for the better after implementing a few different ideas. The ideas are not new, just old ones that worked for centuries until modern so-called professionals chucked them out for 'new ideas'.

There's something else you need to know. Training your child begins with you, not your child. It starts first with Mum and Dad. This book is as much for you, Dad, as it is for Mum. It will help you become a part of the solution and not a part of the problem.

Let's face it; Mum is probably the one spending most time with her toddler. You're working hard at your job. Mum has the greatest opportunity to influence and train the child. Your biggest job, then, is to support Mum and assist in any way you can. Here are some tips in how to do that.

3 things you need to do...

UNDERSTAND the plays

SUPPORT the troops

LEAD BY EXAMPLE as all good captains should.

Terrific Toddlers

UNDERSTAND: Just like players working together in a sports team, you need to understand the methods in this book and the mindset behind them so that you and your wife are on the same team, working the same plays together, and not working against each other.

You should know what character qualities she is focusing on right now, why she is training it, and how she is training it. You initiate a 10-minute catch-up time each day and ask your wife how it's going, what progress has been made today, are there any new developments? If you are like-minded in this you will be working together to achieve a good result more quickly with less pain along the way.

SUPPORT: OK, assuming Mum now knows that you understand what has to be done and why and how, now she needs your encouragement to do the hard stuff. Training moral character consistently day in day out on top of cooking, cleaning, feeding and nappy changes thrown in for good measure is a hard task. It does not make for an exciting, mentally stimulating day. It's just plain hard work, but enormously rewarding in the life of your child, and for you as proud parents.

You must emotionally support and encourage your wife. Remind her that she's not just the mother of your child, but the beautiful woman you married and are still in love with. Your kids are NOT the centre of the universe, yours, hers or theirs. Take her out on regular date nights, and give her some breaks, e.g. time off to be with friends or do her own thing without kids around.

LEAD BY EXAMPLE: Dad, you not may be around Toddler all day like Mum, but you are still the head of the home, and Toddler needs to see and know that Dad's standards are exactly the same as Mum's standards. Toddler needs to see Dad picking up the teaching and training ball.

Terrific Toddlers

Dad must show self-control just as it is expected of Toddler. Toddler also needs to see Dad demonstrating kindness and sharing. Most importantly, Toddler needs to see that the most important person in Dad's life IS NOT TODDLER, but MUM.

To conclude, I want to encourage you to read or re-read ALL of this book, and try to understand as much of the whys and hows as you can. Discuss these with your wife as often as necessary to get a handle on it all. You need to be a team player and the Captain, Dad.

Have fun!

The rewards are awesome!

Terrific Toddlers

Terrific Toddlers Two

So how do we avoid the 'messes' on our pristine white carpet?

By being positive in our words, actions and behaviour.

By managing our anger, and always speaking quietly and politely. By calmly and consistently applying consequences.

By implementing a flexible into our toddler's day.

By focusing on the root cause, not just the symptoms.

These years can be terrific.

However, we can do far more than avoid 'messes' on our carpet. We can build a beautiful home filled with lasting treasures.

In Terrific Toddlers Two we will go beyond simply avoiding the usual toddler frustrations and tantrums.

I will explain the most joyful part of parenting. Teaching your toddler all the positive virtues to overfill their little hearts with goodness. I love it!

We will look at HOW to help your toddler to share, be kind, be gentle, to have his siblings as best friends, to be helpful, to be cheerful, to think of others, to be patient, ... and more.

You'll love it!

Terrific Toddlers

Terrific Toddlers

Terrific Toddlers